SEX POSITIONS

Become A Master At Climax Sex Through Advanced Sex Positions With Pictured Tips And Techniques

Scott Francisco

Table of Contents

Introduction 1
Chapter One: Why Regular Sexual Climax Is Important 2
Chapter Two: Spicing Up Your Sex Life 7
Chapter Three: How To Turn Your Partner On Sexually 15
Chapter Four: Coming Clean About Dirty Talk 20
Chapter Five: Sex Positions 25
Conclusion 61

Introduction

Thank you for taking the time to download this book: Sex Positions.

This book covers the topic of Sex Positions, and will teach you how to master an advanced sex life for intimate, climax sex. This book contains 40 sexual positions that will drive you wild and leave you and your partner begging for more.

At the completion of this book you will have a good understanding of Sex Positions and be able to use and master these positions to reach climax sex. The Positions range from Beginner, Intermediate and mainly Advanced. Start simple and work your way up to mastery and enjoy the adventure of experiencing new, challenging and exciting positions.

Once again, thanks for downloading this book, I hope you find it to be helpful!

Chapter One: Why Regular Sexual Climax Is Important

Sexual climax is the goal of sexual activity, but did you know that there are plenty of other benefits of regular sexual pleasure and climax? Plenty of scientific studies have measured and attested to the various advantages of regular sex and climax to a person's health and well-being. Not only does sex feel good, but it also has many other positive contributions and enhancements to your life.

Sex improves heart health. Healthy, pleasurable sex that gets your blood pumping and causes a lot of physical exertion has much of the same cardiovascular health benefits of exercise or other physical activities. According to a study published in the *American Journal of Cardiology* in January of 2015, men who had sex at least twice a week had a significantly decreased risk of developing cardiovascular diseases, such as heart attack or stroke, compared to men who only had sex once a month or even less.

For people who have no heart problems, regular and vigorous sexual activity is completely safe, according to the guidelines of the American Heart Association which contend that sexual activity poses no heart health threats to individuals who can exercise within a range of 3-5 metabolic equivalents of MET's. MET's calculate how much calories or energy are used during physical activity. Sexual activity at 3 MET's is about the same amount as moderate walking, and sexual activity at 5 MET's is roughly the same as a light aerobic workout program.

For those who are watching their calories, it is interesting to note that the average number of calories burned during a 25-minute sex session is 4 calories for men, and 3 calories for women. So, if you want to burn more calories and have fun doing it, have sex more often and make sure you are both reaching sexual climax!

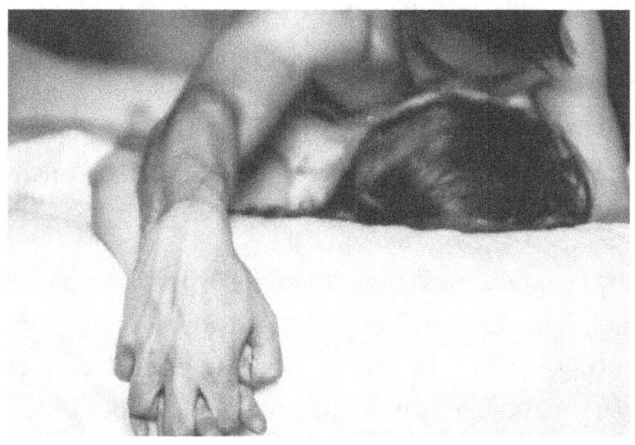

Regular sex helps in stress management. If you are finding yourself stressed out due to the pressures of work or other responsibilities, increasing your sexual activity may help in better managing your stress levels. A study conducted by researchers from the University of Pittsburgh and the University of North Carolina found that among premenopausal women, direct body contact with their husbands or partners raised the levels of the hormone oxytocin in the body. Oxytocin, also monikered the 'love hormone', helps an individual to feel good, or to have the tendency to become more generous or nurturing towards their partner.

Sex has also been found to increase the level of endorphins and other mood-boosting hormones in the body and lower the blood pressure, thus helping an individual to better calm down and regain serenity in a stressful situation. The lowered blood pressure and increased mood-boosting hormone levels have been monitored not only among people having sexual intercourse, but even among those having non-penetrative sexual activity or even masturbation.

Sex may reduce prostate cancer risk among men. In the December 2016 edition of the *European Urology* journal, a study was published showing a possible link between frequent male ejaculation and lower risk of developing prostate cancer. The study found that among those men who ejaculated at least 21 times a month, the risk of prostate cancer was 20 percent lower than among men who only ejaculated 4 to 7 times each month.

Among women, sex may help with menstrual cramp pain. Many women have had to deal with occasional or frequent menstrual cramps during their monthly period. Menstrual cramps, or dysmenorrhea, can range from mild episodes to unbearable discomfort, and may even come with vomiting, nausea, or diarrhea. Many couples are not used to the idea of sexual activity during menstruation, but several studies have found a link between sex and menstrual cramp pain relief.

This pain relief for women occurs when orgasm is reached and more blood rushes to the uterus, thus helping to ease the menstrual pain. During sexual climax, the female body also releases many chemicals and hormones that are natural pain killers, thus helping the body better manage menstrual pain. The effects have been found to be the same for both intercourse and masturbation among women.

Sexual climax improves your sleep. If you have ever wondered why you feel like dozing off after a particularly pleasurable sex session, this is because the orgasm releases a hormone called prolactin in the body. This hormone has the effect of calming your body, relaxing your mind, and helping to make you sleepy. This hormone also induces deeper sleep, so you will wake up feeling more refreshed and energized. So, if you or your partner are having problems getting sleep at night, or you are waking up but still feeling tired, more sex and climax may be particularly beneficial.

Sex strengthens the connection between partners. The emotional, mental, and physical bond between spouses or partners can be greatly enhanced by mutually satisfying and intensely pleasurable bedroom sessions. Both partners will feel the effects of better mood and self-esteem and will then be inclined to share that satisfaction with their partner. In the March 2017 edition of the Psychological Science journal, a study looked at the sexual activity of newlywed couples within a two-week period. It was found that couples reported satisfaction and happiness with each other and with their relationship up to 48 hours after intercourse.

With all these benefits of sexual climax, you and your spouse or partner should make it your goal to enhance your lovemaking sessions and explore each other more intimately, discovering new heights of ecstasy and pleasure you may not have reached yet as a couple. In the next chapter, you will read about some suggestions for spicing up your sex life with the use of creativity and imagination.

Chapter Summary

- Sex has been found to improve cardiovascular health and deliver much of the same benefits as light to moderate aerobic exercise.
- Sexual climax can help lower stress levels by releasing feel-good hormones in the body.
- Men who ejaculate more often are less likely to develop prostate cancer.
- Women experiencing menstrual cramps may find an orgasm particularly helpful in relieving the pain.
- Better sleep is another benefit of a satisfying sexual climax.
- Relationships between spouses or partners become more intimate and connected through a mutually satisfying sex life.

Chapter Two: Spicing Up Your Sex Life

Sex may be one of human beings' favorite activities, but let's face it: it can get monotonous too! If you are doing it the same way over and over again, it tends to feel like a routine that just needs to get over and done with rather than a pleasurable moment between two people in a loving relationship. Many couples don't realize until much later that they have become stuck in a 'rut' or a vicious cycle of repetitive, boring, overused sexual routines that feel more like work than fun.

With a little bit of planning, creativity, imagination and a sense of adventure, you can think of different ways to add spice to your sex life. It is important to communicate clearly with your partner and talk about ways you both can agree to try to reignite that spark in the bedroom and make your sex sessions something to look forward to again.

Sensual massage. If the main culprit behind the sexual rut you are finding yourself in is the hectic schedule and the overworked spouse or partner, a relaxing and sexually-charged massage in the evening may just do the trick. A massage can relax the muscles and get both of you in the mood, and the more touching and intimate stroking is involved, the more aroused both partners will get as the massage goes on. Sensual massage also allows both partners to explore each other's bodies and discover new erogenous zones they may not have been paying attention to. Get the scented candles, take out the oils and lotions, and start the evening with a massage to turn each other on.

Experiment with clothing. Heighten the anticipation through suggestive clothing or seductive underwear. The foreplay should start at the beginning of the day, with both partners sending hints or messages in anticipation of the night's lovemaking. Wearing sexier-than-usual clothing throughout the day can help in getting both of you in the mood and looking forward to tearing each other's clothes off in the evening.

Do it somewhere new. Perhaps your sexual sessions need a change of venue or scenery to become exciting again. Take it out of the bedroom and do it somewhere more spontaneous, such as the kitchen countertop, the hot tub or infinity pool outside, maybe even the shower or bathtub. If you're feeling kinky, try a quickie in the garage or the patio. The excitement of possibly being seen by your neighbors can add thrill to the lovemaking. If you live in a high-rise condo or apartment building, the elevator or the basement parking are possible adventure spots also; just make sure they don't have CCTV cameras.

Introduce sex toys and adult fantasies. You can start this one by going to a sex toy store or adult novelty shop together. Talk about each other's fantasies and pick some sex toys you can both get dirty with, such as dildos, vibrators, cock rings, and other gadgets. The new sensations and kinky innovations will definitely add spark to your bedroom romps.

Try some roleplay. Do you and your spouse or partner enjoy spy movies? Pretend you are both undercover agents meeting at a secret hotel room for a clandestine affair. How about a little bit of BDSM? Unleash your inner Christian Grey and Anastasia Steele and try some whips, handcuffs, blindfolds, and rough play (all consensual, of course). Just make sure to have a safe word!

Get creative with sexual positions. It's easy to just revert to positions you have gotten used to doing, but the level of pleasure and sensations will ramp up to a new level when you decide to try new sex positions and techniques. Start with just learning one new position each week, gradually increasing until you have a whole new arsenal of positions and have tested your limits as far as flexibility, endurance, and stamina. You can consult time-tested guides such as the Kama Sutra for added inspiration. There are plenty of sex positions included in the coming chapters of this book, of course!

Fool around in public. Public exhibitionism is a major turn-on for a lot of people. There is a level of danger and excitement that comes with it, but you should also be careful not to get cited for indecency or public scandal. There's ways to get around it, of course, such as a discreet hand job or fingering under the table at a restaurant, or some heavy petting at the theater. How about a quickie at your partner's office, or a rendezvous at the local library? Again, watch out for CCTV cameras.

Extend the foreplay. Foreplay should not be hurried or rushed through. Remember, women usually take longer to reach a full state of sexual arousal, and extended foreplay will increase her pleasure while also heightening his arousal and making the eventual climax more intense. Instead of jumping straight to the intercourse, stretch out the foreplay session up to a half-hour before going for the main course, and you will immediately feel the difference.

Try blindfolded oral sex. Oral sex is an integral part of foreplay, but what if you turn it up a notch by removing line of sight and relying solely on other senses? When one partner is blindfolded while the other performs oral sex, sensations are heightened and there is the additional twist of not knowing where the mouth will go next. Mutual blindfolded oral sex is also a must-try, as you both tend to feel and explore more with your hands, mouth, lips, and tongue.

Get dirty with words. Words and messages can be used to heighten the anticipation and liven up the actual lovemaking. Throughout the day, you can send each other explicit messages, detailing what you are looking forward to doing to each other later that night. If you are at dinner, whispering to your spouse or partner that you are not wearing underwear or are already completely aroused can heighten the anticipation (you might even end up having a quickie in the washroom). The more you arouse each other verbally throughout the day, the more exciting the actual sex will be in the evening, and you will also become more attuned to each other's pleasure points and turn-ons.

Make it more appetizing. Sex can be a literally appetizing experience with the use of food. Popular options include chocolate, whipped cream, ice cream, strawberry or chocolate syrup or fruits. What you can do is place the food in an area of your body that you would like your partner to give additional attention to, and vice versa. You may also want to incorporate ice cubes for heightened pleasure, or even body shots (tequila and vodka are great for this).

Watch some porn as a couple. A lot of people already view porn on the Internet, but many couples find it awkward or uncomfortable to view porn together. However, once you have tried it and have found some flicks you both enjoy watching, you may end up being so thoroughly turned on that the porn flick just ends up playing in the background while you and your partner do the deed yourselves. Porn can also be used as a creative inspiration for when you want to try new positions or would like to experiment with role-playing or new sex spots.

Use the mirror or film yourselves. If you have not tried it before, watching yourselves having sex and climaxing can be an intense experience. Mirrors may be used strategically for this, so you can see each other's movements and facial expressions; you may even want to try having a mirror installed on the ceiling of your bedroom for an even better perspective. As far as filming yourself and your partner, this can get quite tricky as there is always the risk of your sex tape ending up somewhere it should not be. If you are using your smartphone to film yourselves, make sure to disconnect it from the Internet first so it does not automatically get backed up on the cloud, and then delete the video as soon as you have watched it.

Play games. Sexy, kinky adult games can get you both in the mood for some intense action. Sexy games may be incorporated into your foreplay. Some popular adult games include Strip Poker, Time Bomb (using a timer set to different intervals for kissing, oral sex, fondling, or other activities besides penetration), Sex Fantasy Truth or Dare, Strip Beer Pong, and Naked Pillow Fight (with the loser being punished by performing a sexual act for the winner).

These are just some suggestions for spicing up your sexual escapades and discovering a whole new side of yourself and your partner. In the next chapter, you will read about helpful hints for turning your partner on and getting him or her more excited for sex.

Chapter Summary

- If done according to routine, sex can become monotonous, so you and your partner should think of ways to mix it up.
- A massage is both relaxing and arousing at the same time.
- Suggestive and overtly sexual clothing can be a major turn-on for your partner, and also increase your self-esteem and anticipation.
- Sometimes, just changing your venue can do a lot to rekindle the sexual excitement.
- Sex toys and adult gadgets may be added to the bedroom for new explorations.
- Roleplay is popular among many couples and is an effective and creative way of bringing some new experiences to the sex.
- Various sexual positions should also be studied and tried so you can increase your ammunition.
- Foreplay can be extended for as long as you would like to increase the arousal and anticipation, thus also causing more intense climax.
- A little bit of public display can be very exhilarating, so long as you don't get caught.
- Use blindfolds during oral sex so the other senses are heightened.
- Talking dirty is another popular way to enhance the sexual experience.
- Food items may be added to the mix for more adventure.
- Couples have the option of watching porn together for creative inspiration or just to get turned on.

- The mirror, phone, tablet, or laptop may be used to film yourselves and watch what you both look like.
- Look for sexy games that will make the sex session kinkier.

Chapter Three: How To Turn Your Partner On Sexually

Men and women are wired differently in so many ways, and when it comes to sexuality, there are many contrasts as it pertains to what men and women respond to. In general, men are visually stimulated, while women respond more to touch. Of course, both males and females can be sexually excited by both sight and touch, but you can more quickly get a man's attention through visual cues, and a woman's attention through physical signals.

For men, here are some suggestions for turning your wife or female partner on sexually:

Give her a long, lingering embrace. A woman likes to feel her partner wrapped around her body. It gives her a sense of reassurance and lets her know that you care about her total being. Your partner will be more sexually ready if embraced constantly.

Communicate to her how you feel. A woman likes to hear or read your romantic words and how much you adore her. You can do this by telling her you love her and explaining all the reasons *why* you do, no matter how small or trivial they may seem. Your partner will also love getting love notes or little romantic cards from you telling her how special she is to you. This is a turn-on for most women.

Look for different areas of her body to kiss and caress. From time to time, give your wife or partner a kiss in an area of her body that may not always be getting attention, such as her shoulders, nape, neck, hips, knees, or stomach. The unfamiliar sensation will turn her on rather quickly.

Ask her to give you orders during foreplay. If you are initiating sex and commencing with foreplay, let her know that you are at her beck and call, and you will follow her direct orders. This will encourage her to open up and verbalize what she likes sexually and what gives her pleasure, and also gives you tips for next time.

Pull her close to you in public. A woman is attracted to a man who is stronger and more dominant than her and is not afraid to mark his territory even in front of other people. When you are at a restaurant or a social gathering, pull her close to you by guiding her with your hands around her waist and back, with your pelvis touching her and your eyes directly in contact. This turns a female on right away.

Give her your full attention. When she is sharing about her day, letting you know about her plans for tomorrow, or just talking to you about random stuff, pay close attention and let your woman know that she has your undivided attention. This is an instant thrill to most women.

Practice your oral sex skills. According to the book *The Case of the Female Orgasm*, written by Elisabeth Lloyd and representing over 80 years of research and 33 analytical studies, only 25% of women are able to achieve orgasm from vaginal intercourse only. The odds are greater when it comes to oral sex, so if you want her to achieve sexual climax, cunnilingus or female oral sex should be practiced. You will need to pay attention to her clitoris as this has up to 8,000 nerve endings and is the center of female sexual pleasure. Encourage your partner to let you know what feels good to her and make it your goal to send waves of ecstasy through her body each time you go down on her.

Meanwhile, for women who want to turn on their husband or male partner sexually, here are some helpful hints:

In a public setting, touch him naughtily and seductively. If you are in a social gathering or a restaurant, use your fingertips to lightly trace his arms, lower back, thigh, knee, or chest. This will feel very naughty for both of you, and the surprising gesture will turn him on instantly. Your man will also go crazy if you are walking side by side and you give his buttocks a sudden squeeze, or you lightly brush your body against his manhood.

Buy sexy lingerie. The more suggestive and out-of-the-ordinary, the more you will get his attention and excite him sexually. Men are visual creatures, and the sight of you in a particularly sexy lingerie will trigger his imagination and make him nuts. The sheer material of the lingerie will also be a turn-on for you.

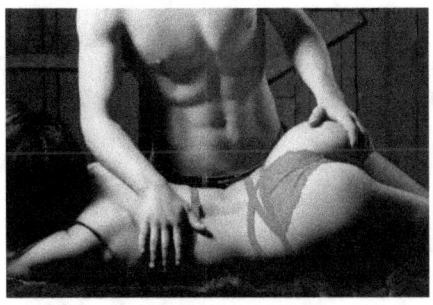

Give him a head and shoulder massage. If your man is coming home tired and stressed out from work - a scalp massage will relax his mind, soothe his nerves, and also arouse him sexually. You can give him a head massage while sitting next to each other on the couch, or a shoulder massage as he sits at the dinner table at the end of the day. Sensual and lingering strokes should start at the back of his neck, close to the ears, moving up to the scalp, and then working down to his nape and shoulders. You can add more sexual tension by giving him light kisses or licking his ears towards the end of the massage.

Present him with a strip show. Why do men like going to strip clubs or burlesque shows? Because men are easily aroused by sexual images and the female form. Your husband or partner may have already seen you in the nude plenty of times before, but if you add a little mystery and sensuality to the process, you can make it all seem new to him again. Give him a little striptease, perhaps even a lap dance if you are up to it, slowly removing your articles of clothing one by one but not letting him touch you. This will drive him crazy and make him anticipate being able to touch you again.

Take a shower or bath together. Surprise your husband or partner by joining him in the shower or prepping the tub for when he gets home so you can both get lathered up, relaxed, and ready for action. Make it even more sensual by soaping him up yourself and paying particular attention to his pleasure areas. You may not make it to the bed once it gets all hot and heavy in the shower.

In the next chapter, you will read all about one ingredient of sexual creativity and pleasure that is sure to ignite anticipation for both partners – dirty talk.

Chapter Summary

- Women like to be embraced and reassured physically and verbally.
- To turn your wife or female partner on, look for new areas of her body to kiss.
- Let her know that she can give you direct orders during fore-play, so you know what feels good to her.
- Women are turned on when they have the man's full attention in public, and when they are held close to the man in a territorial way.
- Oral sex skills should be perfected.
- Naughty and seductive touches in public will turn a man on sexually.
- To excite your man, wear sexy lingerie or give him a sexy strip show.
- A head and shoulder massage will relax your husband or partner and also get him aroused.
- A nice, long bath or shower together is always a turn-on for both partners.

Chapter Four: Coming Clean About Dirty Talk

During the heat of sexual activity, many couples enjoy kinky, dirty talk. People enjoy taking on a whole new persona or unleashing their wild side while having sex, and dirty talk is one of the most erotic ways to let go of all control and just allow oneself to immerse in the pleasure. Dirty talk is more than just a wild effect of uninhibited sexual passion, however. It can be used to liven up your sex life and allow both partners to become more comfortable in communicating their sexual wants and desires.

There are many benefits to dirty sex talk, foremost of which is the fact that for both men and women, the brain is the most powerful sex organ, even more than the reproductive organs. This is because the brain controls the human sex drive, and if you want to heighten the body's sexual response and awareness, you should target the brain first, which is precisely what dirty talk does. During dirty talk, various areas or regions of the brain are being activated sexually at the same time that the body is being stimulated physically, and this creates a total experience connecting the mind and body.

For women, in particular, dirty talk stimulates the region of the brain known as the amygdala which is where many feelings of excitement and pleasure stem from. So when kinky talk is happening during sex, the mental stimulation heightens sexual pleasure and makes both partners more responsive to each other while also giving way or verbalizing fantasies that may be explored.

The verbalization of these fantasies and desires is an important component to becoming a better lover and enjoying sexual climax more. When dirty talk is occurring, it often revolves around things that either partner want to do or be done to them which would give pleasure. This makes it easier for the other person to understand what makes his or her spouse or partner tick, rather than guessing or going by trial-and-error.

In a study published in 2012 by the *Journal of Social and Personal Relationships*, it was found that the more comfortable people are about talking about sex, the more satisfying their sex lives will be as well. The study found that couples who were communicating to each other during sex were more likely to have greater sexual satisfaction and enhanced sexual climax.

Dirty talk does not have to happen within the bedroom or during sexual intercourse, of course. The pleasure of kinky talk can be extended throughout the day, making it a form of foreplay that lasts for many hours and keeps both partners anticipating what will happen later on. For instance, you and your spouse or partner may enjoy sending each other sexually explicit messages on SMS, chat, or voicemail, letting the other person know what you intend to do when you get home. This keeps both of you excited and looking forward to seeing each other at the end of the day.

When couples are used to talking dirty to each other both in the bedroom and elsewhere, they become more intimately connected to each other and comfortable in their own sexuality, thus paving the way for more open and frank discussions of what each other likes. This strengthens the bond between spouses or partners and also enriches the relationship as a whole, with the added benefit of enhancing sexual pleasure and climax as both partners let go of their inhibitions and unleash their hidden persona.

When incorporating dirty talk into your relationship, be sensitive to each other's needs and preferences. Some people, for instance, may like being called terms such as "slut" or "whore" during sex, but not necessarily in other settings especially publicly. Other individuals, on the other hand, would prefer that dirty sex talk avoid potentially offensive or derogatory remarks, choosing instead to focus on explicit sexual plans and positions. Whatever the case may be for you as a couple, make sure to accommodate your partner's requests and also be ready to accede or agree to any limits the other person sets.

Come clean to your partner about what you do and don't like about dirty talk. The comfort and pleasure of your partner should be foremost in any sexual adventure or exploration, including kinky language used with each other. Any form of dirty talk that excites you both and enhances your sexual climax should be welcomed as part of a healthy and vibrant sexual relationship, allowing both partners to become more confident and to become more intimately connected to each other.

In the next chapter, you will read about various sexual positions ranging from beginner, intermediate, to advanced which you you'll be interested in trying with your spouse or partner.

Chapter Summary

- Dirty talk allows couples to open up and become more comfortable with their sexual desires.
- The brain is the most powerful sexual organ, and dirty language unleashes and enhances sexual climax by targeting and stimulating the brain.
- Kinky language allows partners to learn more about each other's sexual turn-ons.
- Dirty talk doesn't have to be confined to the bedroom, as it can also occur throughout the day as a form of foreplay and for keeping each other excited.

Chapter Five: Sex Positions

Becoming a better lover and mastering sexual climax can be likened to an art form that requires lots of practice and constant skills improvement. If you really want to become a better sexual partner, you should be open to learning new techniques or positions and add them to your current line-up of favorite sexual styles.

Beginner Sex Positions

First, here are some basic sex positions:

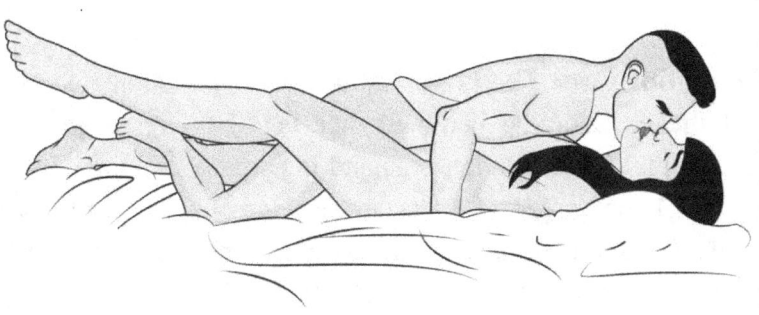

Missionary. The Missionary position is still the most popular among couples. In this style, the woman lies on her back, and the man gets on top of her, penetrating her from the front. The woman can then lift her knees close to her chest during penetration, or even rock her hips back and forth for increased sensation. The Missionary position allows easy access to the female clitoris, which can be stimulated by either the male or the female during penetration. The female can also grab the man's back, hips, or buttocks during intercourse.

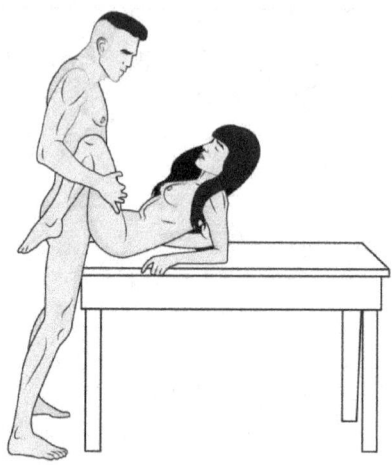

Dangling Over The Edge. In this position, the female lies on her back at the edge of the bed with her legs hanging, then the male positions himself between her legs and penetrates, holding up her hips or legs for better angle. This is an easy position for both partners, especially for the man, because he does not need to support his body weight on his upper body or arms. If the bed is lower than desired, pillows may be placed under the woman's hips, or the man can kneel in between her legs. Couples who like deep penetration and more forceful thrusting motions during intercourse will particularly enjoy this style.

Woman On Top. For this style, the man will sit down upright with his legs out in front of him. The woman gets on top of him, straddling his body between her legs. She then takes his penis and lowers her vagina down to commence penetration. The woman is in control of the motion, speed, and angle of thrusting, and can try different variations such as circular grinding, moving her hips up and down, or leaning forward or back. The woman on top position is great for couples where the man has a larger penis compared to her smaller vagina, as it allows her to take control and let her vagina expand before the penis thrusts deeper. The clitoris is also easily stimulated as it rubs between her partners stomach during thrusts.

Sitting In A Chair. If you want to try a position outside the bed, use a sturdy chair for this one (preferably one with no wheels or armrests). The man sits in the chair or bed like a chair, and the woman gets on top of him, facing him while straddling him between her legs. She lowers himself onto him, controlling the penetration, and move up and down or grind in a circular motion. The sitting position may also be done on the couch, but the female will be on her knees instead of her legs on the ground. This style gives the woman total control of the depth, speed, and angle, and is also a great hip, back, and leg workout for her. The clitoris is easily accessible for manual stimulation.

Tight Squeeze. In this position, the woman lies down on her stomach with her legs straight and spread slightly apart. Then, the man gets on top of her, his body stretched over hers and his weight supported by his elbows or hands. The man's legs should be positioned outside the woman's as he penetrates her, and then she can cross her legs or ankles during intercourse. This position is great for couples who really want to feel a lot of friction and deep thrusting. During penetration, the man can also lick or kiss the woman's ears, neck, or shoulders. This style is great for those nights when you are both physically tired but still amorous and want to have sex without expending too much energy. Placing a pillow under the woman's waist also helps G-Spot stimulation and easy access.

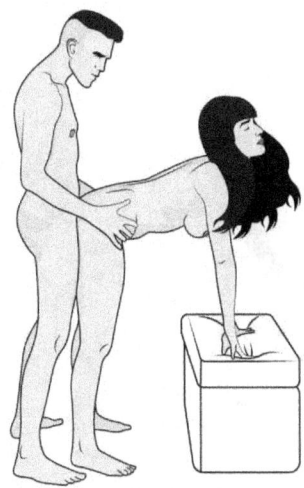

Hot Rod. If you are getting down and dirty in the shower, try this simple shower sex position. The woman stands on her feet and bends her back towards her toes leaning on the wall, seat/bench or her knees for support. The man then penetrates her from behind, grabbing her waist to pull her close to him. This position can be done as you are both soaping up or rinsing off, with lots of water and soap suds for added eroticism and lubrication. This style is also great for those morning lovemaking sessions before you both head out for the day.

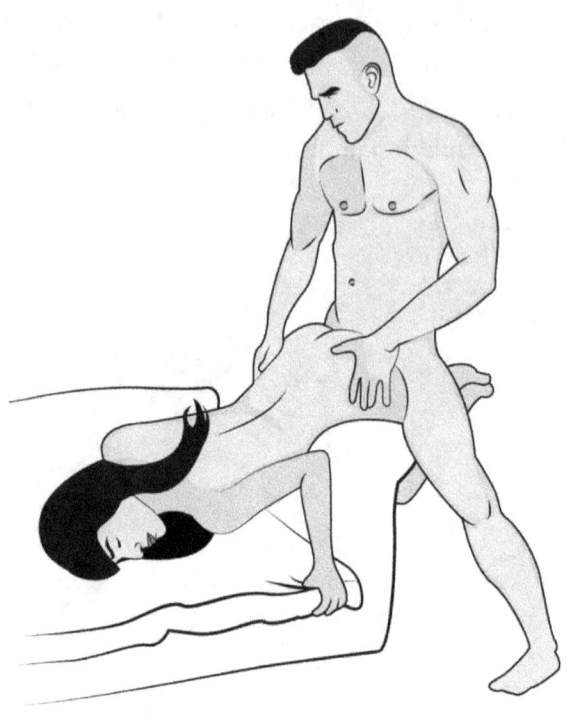

Bed Spread. This technique is a variation of the Dangling Over The Edge position. This time, the woman lies down on her stomach over the edge of the bed or couch, her legs dangling or feet on the floor. The man gets between her legs and commences penetration. The man can also lift both legs up, holding them apart and begin thrusting. The bed spread position allows for deeper penetration, and the angle of the penis will increase the woman's pleasure as well. In this technique, the man will have a great view of her back and buttocks as he penetrates.

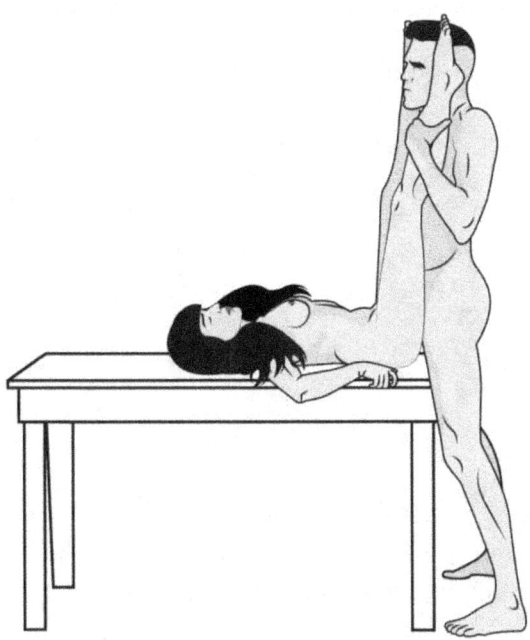

Sexy Scissors. Want to incorporate your desk, countertop, or kitchen table into the lovemaking? This erotic position is a must-try. The woman lies down on the surface with her hips on the edge, then she raises her legs up to a 90-degree angle. The man holds her ankles in place, standing between her legs, penetrating her then crossing and spreading the woman's legs similar to the movement of scissors. This creates a very tight wave of sensations for both partners, and both the man and woman have a full view of each other in an intensely erotic but easy sexual position.

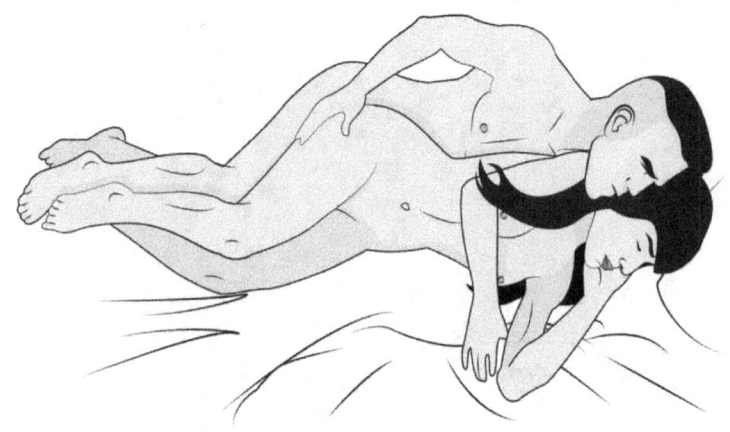

Spooning. Most people think of spooning as something couples do after lovemaking, but this cuddling position can also be a sexual position for beginners. With the woman lying on her side, the man wraps his arms around her, lying on his side next to her, as he penetrates her vagina with his penis and thrusts from behind. Both partners feel very close to each other because they are cuddling while having intercourse, and it is also very stress-free and relaxing for both partners. The man is free to stimulate her breasts or clitoris with his hands, or her ears, neck, shoulders, or nape with his tongue and lips. A variation of this position is facing each other, legs wrapped around each other's bodies.

Doggy Style. This is one of the more popular sex positions for beginners, and it is fun and erotic at the same time. In fact, many men count doggy style as their favorite technique. In this position, the woman is on all fours on the bed as the man positions himself behind her and enters her vagina from behind. As she gets more comfortable, she can arch her back to allow the man to penetrate deeper. In this position, some naughty butt-slapping and hair-pulling can occur, and the man is also free to reach around and play with her clitoris as he is thrusting from behind. There are quite a few variations you can also try, such as the woman lying face down on the bed rather than propped up on her elbows, with just her lower body raised up.

Ready for more challenging sex techniques? Here are intermediate sex positions to try:

Intermediate Sex Positions

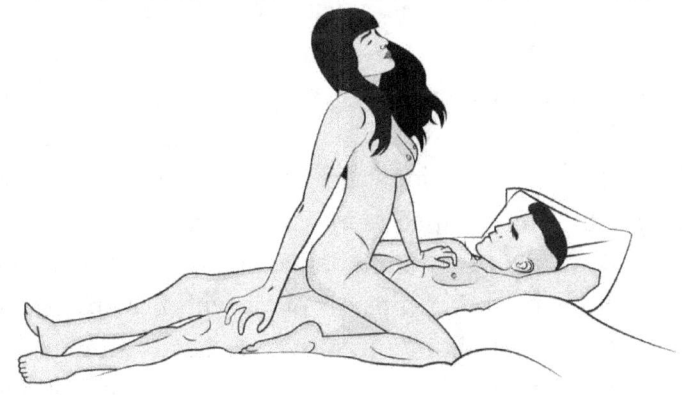

Cowgirl. This sex position is achieved with the man lying on his back towards the edge of the bed, then sliding his head and shoulders down to the floor. Then, the woman straddles him and lowers her vagina on his penis, taking control of the penetration and thrusting motions. In this technique, the blood will rush to the man's head and increase sexual climax, while the woman is free to control the tempo as she wishes and also stimulate her clitoris or other pleasure zones as she moves up and down or in a circular motion.

Reverse Cowgirl. This is a variation of the Woman On Top position, or the Cowgirl. In Reverse Cowgirl, the man lies on his back, then the woman straddles his hips, facing toward his feet, and kneels as she lowers her vagina onto his penis. Once inserted, she begins to ride his penis in an upward, sideways, or circular motion. The Reverse Cowgirl also allows the woman to either lean backward or forward to change the angle of the penetration depending on what feels better for her. The man holds on to her hips, or plays with her breasts, back, or clitoris, while the woman is free to move her hands all over her body or reach under and play with his scrotum during penetration. If the man wants to take charge he can bend his knees and hold himself up with his hands and arms, lifting his buttocks up and penetrating his partner from behind.

Pretzel Dip. This position combines the deep thrusts and penetration of the doggy style but with the partners able to face each other. The man kneels on the bed while the woman is lying on her side. Then, he straddles one of her legs while she beds her other leg around his waist. The man penetrates her vagina deeply. In this position, the man can stimulate her clitoris or other body parts with his hands, or even pull out his penis and rub it along her clitoris for sexual climax.

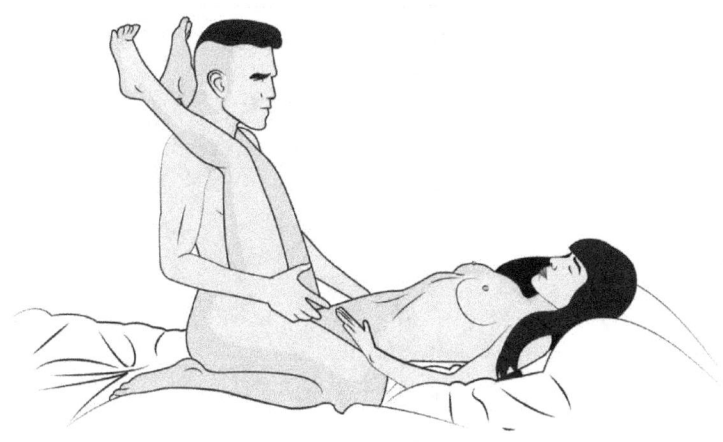

Anvil. Also called the shoulder holder, this is quite similar to the missionary position but with a bit more flexibility required. The woman lies on her back, legs apart, as the man kneels between her legs. He then raises her legs, placing her calves over his shoulders as he penetrates her slowly and thrusts from side-to-side or upward and downward. In this position, the head and the shaft of the penis will be directly stimulating the front area of the woman's vagina, causing more intense sensations and climax. This technique also allows her to roam her hands all over his body as he is inside her. A variation of this position is the woman placing her feet against his chest so she can have more control of the depth and tempo of penetration.

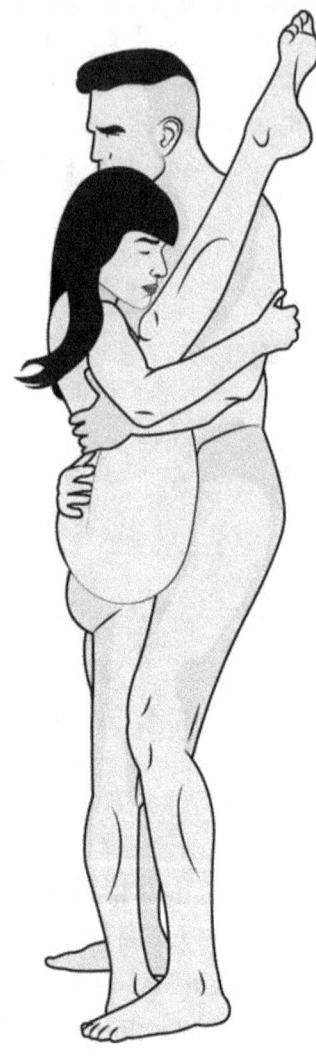

Ballet Dancer. If you are trying outdoor sex, this position should be on your list. Both partners stand facing each other, and the woman raises one leg and wraps it around the man's thigh/buttocks or if flexible enough, on top of his shoulder, while holding on to his shoulders or torso for support. The man wraps his arms around her and enters from the front. If needed he can also support her raised leg with one arm, or lift her leg over his shoulder him self. This standing position is also ideal for shower sex. The penetration is deeper and the angle can be adjusted easily, and this technique is very intimate especially as the woman can move her hands all over his backside while being penetrated.

Aquaman's Delight. Do you have a pool or hot tub outside and want to have a quickie while taking a dip? This technique is very similar to the Ballet Dancer, but with the added comfort of buoyancy in the water to help with maintaining the position. Partners stand facing each other as the woman wraps her legs around him and holds on to his shoulders for support, while he penetrates from the front. For couples who want to try sex in public, this position is great because it just looks like you are embracing each other and bobbing up and down with the water current (that is, if you can keep quiet).

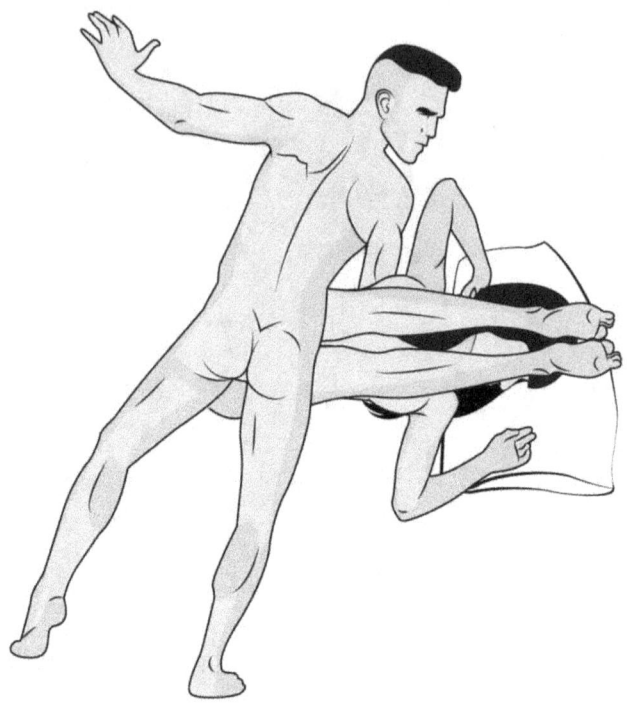

Spork. This position is named after the spoon and fork combination, and is a great entryway to other more advanced sex positions. The woman lies on her back, with one leg raised as the man gets between her legs, penetrating at a 90-degree angle. The woman's legs will look like a spoon-and-fork combination, and both legs can also be raised if she is flexible enough, allowing deeper penetration. The Spork technique leaves the clitoris and the breasts open for manual stimulation from either partner, thus intensifying sexual climax.

Crisscross. Also known as the X Position, this technique is for couples who want to take it slow and gradually build to a more explosive finale. Partners sit on the bed in front of each other, and legs forward. The man will sit across his partner making a T shape, and then lift his right leg over her left leg, while the woman lifts her right leg over his shoulder. He then inserts his penis as they both move closer to each other, then they both lie back as the legs form the letter X. In this position, only shallow thrusts or gyrations of the penis may be done, thus focusing the sensation on the head of the penis and the front wall of the vagina.

The Spider. Couples who like to watch each other's facial expressions during lovemaking will particularly enjoy this technique. The man and woman will sit on the bed, legs toward each other, and their arms supporting their back weight. They come closer as the woman opens her vagina to his penis, her hips between the man's leg while her knees are bent and feet are flat on the bed for support. The man or woman will then rock back and forth. This position is great for moderately athletic and flexible couples, and the man can also caress her buttocks or back during penetration.

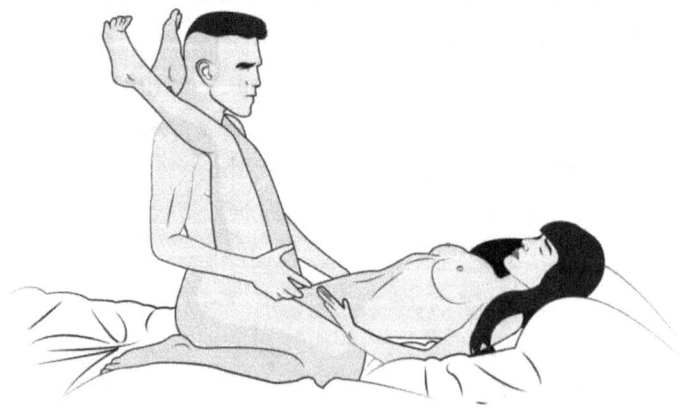

The Fusion. Closely related to The Spider, but with the variation of the woman's legs on the man's shoulders. In this position, the penetration is deeper and the angle elevates the muscular tension around the female pleasure point. The woman can control the thrusting motion and the speed, thus focusing on her pleasure. The man can use one hand to also caress her clitoris during penetration, adding to her sensations.

Swiss Ball Blitz. If you have a stability ball at home, you can use this simple workout equipment to add some bounce to your lovemaking session. The position is similar to the Sitting In A Chair position, but with the added bonus of the stability ball's bouncing motions as he thrusts into her. It's also a great workout for both of you and develops balance and endurance.

Downward Dog. Individuals who like yoga will be familiar with this position which is quite similar to Doggy Style. The woman will kneel down and lie face down on the bed, her legs apart and one hand behind her back. The man kneels between her legs, with one hand taking her arm behind her back, while his other hand holds her head or neck as he thrusts into her. Couples who like to role-play or who would like to try more forceful penetration will enjoy this style.

The Cross. In this position, the woman lies on her stomach with her arms spread out in front of her, and her head lifted up towards him. Her legs are laid out shoulder width apart, and the man is positioned behind her in a vertical angle, on his knees, as he penetrates her from behind. His arms are free to touch and caress her face, head, and breasts, while she is more relaxed. A variation of this technique is for the man to rock the woman forward and back towards him while he kneels in place.

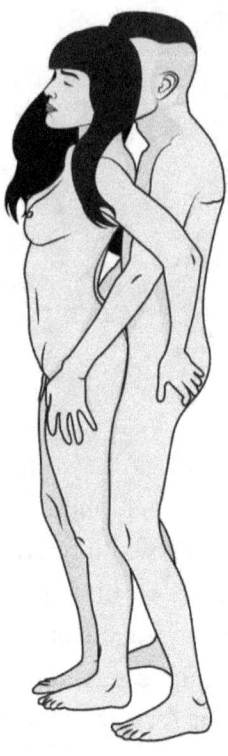

Wall. For couples who want to try sex in other areas of the house or even in other public places, the Wall position should be tried. The man leans back against a wall, door, or other flat, sturdy surface, with his legs spread slightly and forward. The woman will then get in front of him, her back to him, as she slightly leans forward and she places her hands on the man's thighs. He grabs her around the waist and penetrates, thrusting using his hips or rocking her body forward and back. His hands are free to caress her breasts, clitoris, and other pleasure zones, while she is free to play with his scrotum or buttocks while getting penetrated.

Ready to move on to even more challenging techniques? Here are some advanced sex positions for you to try:

Advanced Sex Positions

The Mermaid. If the male partner is particularly strong or the female is light and limber, this position should also be tried. Both partners are standing, with the man's fee together and slightly bent in the knees. She is standing with her back to him as the man holds her by the stomach and lifts her toward him. She then pulls her hands back to lock them under his arms, while bending her knees and moving closer to him, her feet positioned under his buttocks. As he penetrates and moves inside her, he is carrying most of her weight. This position is great for deep vaginal stimulation.

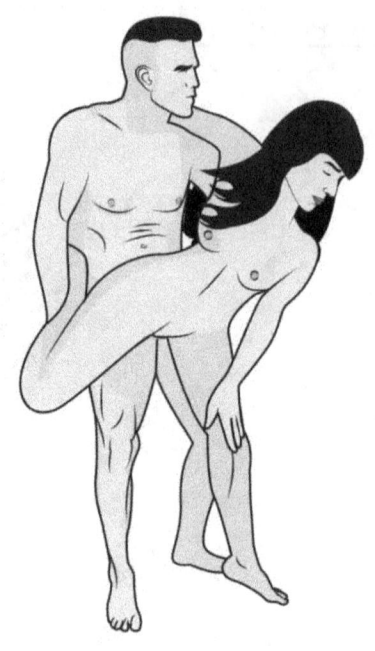

Sagittarius. Yet another standing sexual position, this one combines deep thrusts and clitoral stimulation for maximum pleasure. Man and woman stand next to each other, with the woman facing sideways and on her toes. He pulls an arm around her waist, then with his other arm takes her foot and raises it, bent around the knee, as he penetrates from the side. She can hang on to his shoulders or neck for balance, while touching her breasts or clitoris with her other hand. Kissing, necking, and fondling are all easily performed in this technique.

The Pole. Also known as Thighmaster, this position targets both the inner vagina and the clitoris of the woman and offers the man an erotic view of the woman riding his penis. To try this position, the man lies on his back with one leg bent while the other leg is stretched. The woman then straddles the raised leg with her thigh, lowering her vagina onto the man's penis with her back to him. She will use his knee for support as she begins upward, downward, and circular motions, hence the "Pole" term. In this style, her inner vagina gets maximum stimulation from the penis, while her clitoris rubs against his thigh, thus doubling the sensation.

Squat Thruster. This is also called the Butter Churner and is the other variation of the Waterfall. This time around, it is the female who will experience a blood rush to her head for maximum sexual climax. She lies on her back then raises her legs over her head, as far as she can go. The man then squats over her and lowers himself, entering her from the top as he dips in and out of her. For maximum sensation, it is recommended that the man completely withdraw his penis and then penetrate her fully several times. The rush of blood will intensify the female sensation.

Standing Wheelbarrow. The woman will have to be quite athletic to be able to pull this off. She will lie on her stomach, legs apart, as the man lifts her up by the pelvis and she wraps her legs around his waist. He then enters her from behind, still supporting her waist with his hands, as he begins to thrust in and out of her vagina. There is also a head rush that the female will experience in this style, and this position burns a lot of calories as well.\

Seating Wheelbarrow. If the Standing Wheelbarrow is too difficult at first, try the Seating Wheelbarrow first. The woman lies down on her stomach at the edge of the bed, or bends over on a chair, as the man grabs her waist and pulls her up to him, penetrating from behind while her arms support her weight on the floor. The angle of penetration here is very deep and varied, increasing her stimulation, while her clitoris rubs against his groin. The man gets a perfect view of her backside and buttocks in an erotic and submissive position.

Leapfrog. Couples who like Doggy Style but want to up the ante can try this technique. The woman will stand on her limbs, leaning on her arms and toes, and with her knees and elbows slightly bent. The body is leaning forward and her buttocks are raised and exposed. The man will enter her from the rear, keeping his arms on her buttocks or waist for support and to thrust deeper into her vagina. Leapfrog is great for reaching those deeper crevices of the vagina that are not normally stimulated during penetration.

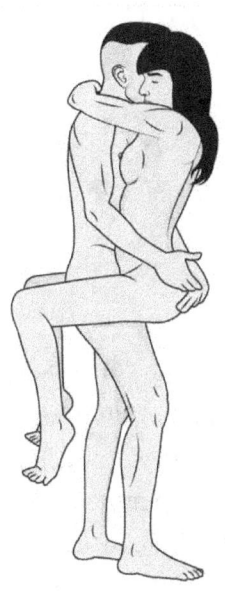

Stand And Carry. If the man has great upper body strength or the woman is light enough for him to carry, this standing position is great for couples who want to try a bit of outdoor sex or exhibitionism (i.e. having sex in front of a hotel window looking out over the city). The man stands upright as the woman wraps her arms around his upper body, then the man lifts her up by her heels. Her weight is supported by his arms as she uses his grip to thrust herself up and down on his penis. Be careful not to be standing too close to any items or furniture you might accidentally topple over when doing this challenging sex position!

The Torch. This is another unique position that does require lots of stamina and balance. The man will kneel and sit along side his feet, making sure his legs are slightly apart. Facing him, the woman sits on his thighs, while her legs are perched on his shoulders, and she holds on to his back for support. She can then throw her head back in sheer abandon as the thrusting begins, with the man moving her body rhythmically and with increasing intensity. The couple are free to also kiss in this position, or the man can roam his tongue around her neck, ears, or breasts, while she can massage his back, stroke his arms, or play with his scrotum during penetration.

The Spin. This is another very unique and adventurous sex position for those who like a good challenge. If the female wants a different ride, this position will literally spin her world around. The man sits up straight with his legs extended straight in front of him as the woman sits on top of him and places his penis inside her. Then, the woman spins around 180 degrees with the man supporting with one hand. This position will be uniquely pleasurable for both partners and the sensations will be starkly different from those of other techniques, but this is also very physically challenging. Also, the woman may feel some nausea if not used to the spinning motion, so the first few tries should be done slowly and gently, allowing her to get used to the 180-degree cycle.

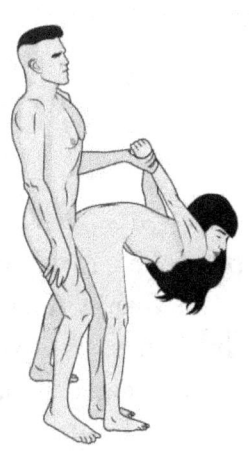

Prison Guard. Thinking of a little bit of rough roleplay? Try this physically challenging position which literally holds the woman hostage. The man will stand to his feet as the woman stands in front of him, her back towards him and her legs apart and knees bent. She bends her body forward and her hands are on her back, while the man then takes her hands by the wrists and inserts his penis from behind, keeping her in place by holding on to her hands. The woman is at the mercy of the man's pounding motions, and this is a good technique for couples who want to go a but further because it is primal and forceful in nature.

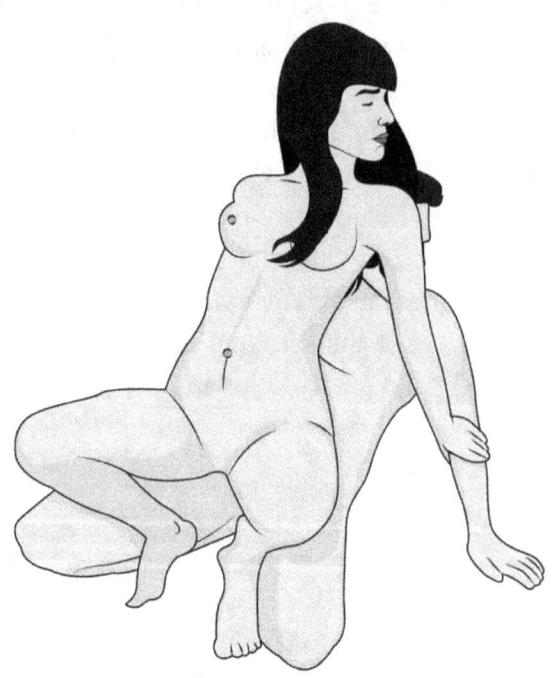

Crucifixion. Partners who like to explore their bodies' limits will want to try this technique. The man will sit down on his feet, leaning backward and resting on his hands. The woman has her back to the man as she sits on his penis, her weight supported by his arms, her legs between his legs and supported by her toes. She can tilt her head backwards towards the man's shoulders, and either the woman moves up and down or the man can also thrust upward during intercourse. This is a great core and arm workout for both partners, and is also highly erotic especially if the woman practices clenching her vagina to make it tighter and send the man to ecstasy.

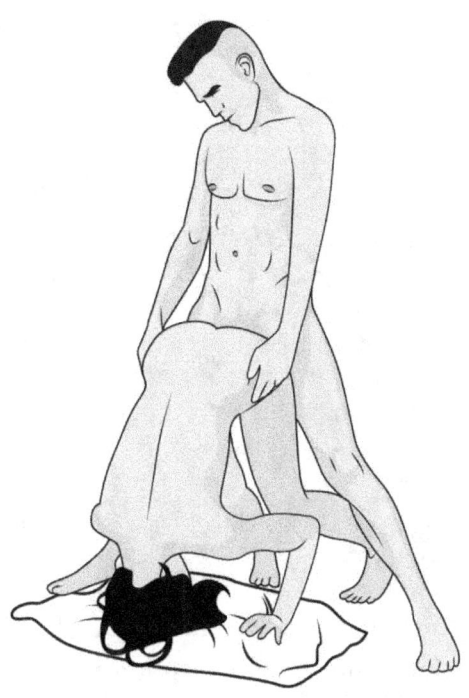

Advanced Leapfrog. The Advanced Leapfrog position combines aspects of many other sex positions such as Doggy Style and Leapfrog. In this style, the man is standing, leaning backwards while holding his partner's waist. The woman will face away from him in a squat position, leaning all the way over in front of her so her head is upside down and she can see behind her. As she sits on his penis and leans forward, she will be able to rock backwards and forwards. With her hands in front of her, she leans forward and backward rhythmically as the man grabs her buttocks to guide the movements. As the tempo is set, he can then move his free hand around her waist to stimulate her groin, breasts, or clitoris. This position allows for very fast thrusts.

Bridge. If the man has great upper body and core strength, and the woman is particularly limber, this position is a must-try. The Bridge position is especially attractive to couples who do yoga together. The man will sit with legs bent at the knees, his arms supporting his weight, as the woman faces him and straddles him, lowering her vagina over his penis, while her legs support her weight. He then penetrates and begins thrusting upward, all while keeping her weight supported by his body, as they try to gain balance and tempo. This is especially strenuous for the man but is very pleasurable for the woman because of the deep penetration angle and the friction of her clitoris against his groin.

Reflection. This very erotic and intimate sex position will make the couple even closer emotionally, listening to each other's breathing and looking into each other's eyes deeply. To achieve this position, the man and woman will kneel in front of each other, their knees connected, as the man bends one of his knees and the woman perches her leg over it. The man embraces the woman around the waist and penetrates her at this angle, while the woman can hold on to his head or shoulders for additional support. The position is great for lots of eye contact and gentle, rhythmic thrusting, with both partners also able to caress each other with their free hands.

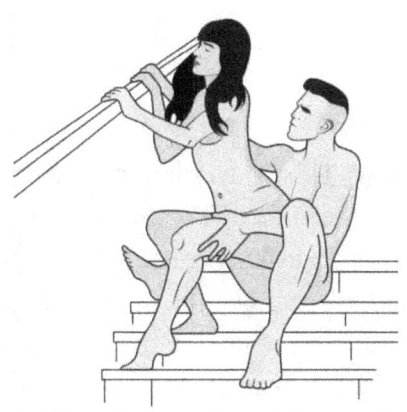

Stairway to Heaven. Take your sex life to the next level using the stairs of your home. In this position, the man sits on the stairs, his legs close together, as the woman stands in front of him, facing away from him, and lowers her vagina onto her penis, her hands on the bannister or wall. She then moves up and down or in circular motion, controlling the thrust and the speed of the penetration. Couples who want to move their sex sessions away from the bedroom can definitely try this position. It's also a great core and quads workout for the woman.

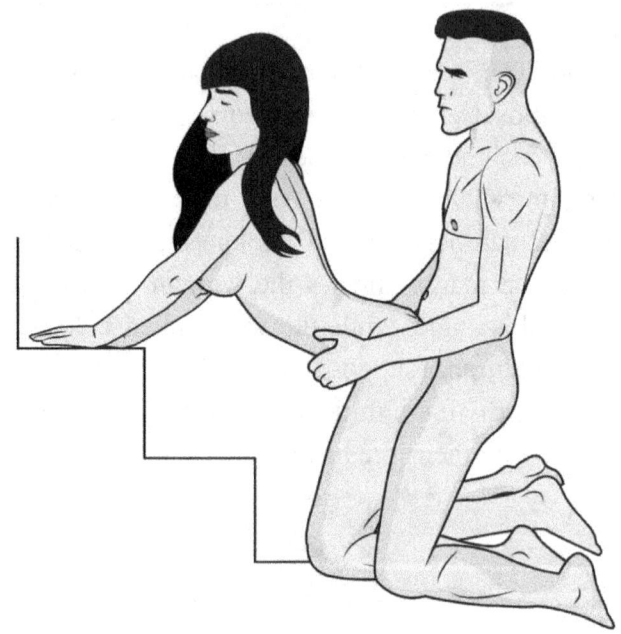

Backstairs Boogy. This is a variation of the Stairway to Heaven, but also making use of the stairs. This time around, the woman kneels on the staircase, and the man kneels behind her, both of them facing the stairs as he enters her from behind. The woman can hold on to the bannister or wall for support, while the man hangs on to her hips as he penetrates her for deeper thrusts. This position is great if your stairs are carpeted, otherwise, be prepared for some knee soreness. This position is great for experimenting with sex in different areas of the house, and for role-playing scenarios as well. The angle of the penetration and the manual stimulation also intensifies the sexual climax for the woman, and the sensation for the man is very similar to Doggy Style.

Chapter Summary

Revisit the key points of the chapter in bullet point format.

- There are different levels of sex positions you can try: Beginner, Intermediate or Advanced.
- It is good to try different sexual positions and get lots of practice so you can become a master at sexual climax.

Conclusion

Thanks again for taking the time to download this book!

You should now have a good understanding of Sex Positions, and be able to use these positions and skills to advance and master your sex life.

If you enjoyed this book, please take the time to leave me a review on Amazon. I appreciate your honest feedback, and it really helps me to continue producing high quality books.

www.ingramcontent.com/pod-product-compliance
Lightning Source LLC
Chambersburg PA
CBHW072111290426
44110CB00014B/1890